W9-BFS-664

INCREDIBLE INSECTS

BEETLES

James E. Gerholdt

Published by Abdo & Daughters, 4940 Viking Drive, Suite 622, Edina, Minnesota 55435.

Printed in the United States.

Cover Photo credit: Peter Arnold, Inc.
Interior Photo credits: James E. Gerholdt pages 5, 7, 8, 11, 12, 13, 18
Peter Arnold pages 9, 15, 17, 19, 21

Edited by Julie Berg

Library of Congress Cataloging-in-Publication Data

Gerholdt, James E., 1943
    Beetles / by James E. Gerholdt.
    p.   cm. — (Incredible Insects)
Glossary and index.
    ISBN 1-56239-481-9
1. Beetles—Juvenile literature. [1. Beetles.] I. Title. II . Series:
Gerholdt, James E., 1943- Incredible Insects.
QL576.2.G47 1995
595.76—dc20   95-1514
                                                   CIP
                                                   AC

Contents

BEETLES

Beetles are one of the 28 insect orders. Insects are arthropods. This means their skeleton is on the outside of their body. They also are ectothermic—they get their body temperature from the environment. There are about 300,000 beetle species. They are found worldwide.

Almost one-third of all animals known to science are beetles (figure 1). About two-fifths of all the insects known to science are beetles (figure 2). Beetles are different from other insects because their hardened front wings form a case for the rear wings. They also have a biting mouth that grabs their food.

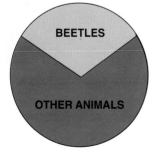

Figure 1.

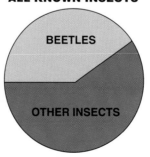

Figure 2.

Top Right: The Atlas beetle from Malaysia has a mouth that can bite.

Bottom Right: The flamboyant flower beetle from Africa has hardened front wings that cover the rear wings.

LIFE CYCLE

All beetles go through a complete metamorphosis. This means there are four stages in their life cycle. They hatch from eggs and spend the first part of their life as a larva, or grub. The mealworms sold in pet or bait shops are beetle larvae!

After a while, the larva goes into a resting stage, called the pupa. The adult beetle emerges from the pupa. Some species, like the chafers, lay only a single egg. Others, like the oil beetles, may lay several thousand.

Right: This king mealworm beetle has just emerged from the pupa.

Left: Mealworms are the larvae of the mealworm beetle.

SIZES

Most beetles are very tiny. Some are small. And some are large enough to be scary! The smallest beetle is only one-hundredth of an inch long (.25 mm). However, most beetles are larger.

Some stag beetles can be 1 1/2 inches (4 cm) long. The Hercules beetle can grow 6.8 inches (17 cm) long. The largest beetle is the Goliath beetle, which can be 8 inches (20 cm) long!

**Right:
This longhorned beetle has a very hard body and is completely black in color.**

**Left:
The longhorned beetle from Minnesota is about 1 inch (2.5 cm) long.**

SHAPES

Beetles have many strange shapes. A few are long and slender, like the click and long-horned beetles. But even these are not as slender as other insects. Some beetles are almost round, like ladybird beetles (or lady bugs) and water beetles. But most are shaped like stag beetles, about twice as long as they are wide.

What really makes beetles look different is their jaws and their antennae. The stag and Atlas beetles have huge jaws. The long-horned beetles have very long antennae.

Like all insects, beetles have three body parts: the head, thorax, and abdomen. They also have six legs, and two antennae.

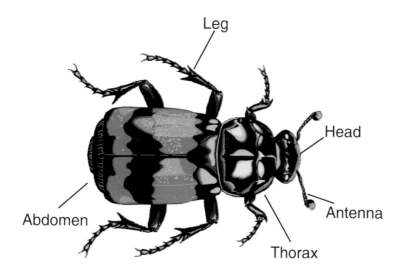

Leg

Head

Antenna

Abdomen

Thorax

Top Right:
The orange-spotted longhorned beetle from Maylaysia has very long antennae.

Bottom Right:
You can see the three body parts on this metallic scarab beetle from Arizona.

COLORS

Many beetles are brightly colored. Other beetles have colors that help them blend in with their surroundings. This is called camouflage. Even a bright green beetle is hard to see if it is on a green plant or moss.

Some beetles look like tree bark, while others are colored like the ground. Some weevils grow fungi and algae on their wing covers. A few species have markings on their abdomen that look like large eyes. These markings help them fool their enemies.

**Right:
The Congo chafer beetle from Africa has markings that look like eyes on the rear of its abdomen.**

**Left:
The longhorned beetle from Minnesota is brightly colored.**

WHERE THEY LIVE

Beetles live in many different habitats. The larvae usually remain hidden until they change into an adult beetle.

Some, like the tiger beetles, live under rocks. Others, like the ladybird beetles, live on plants and help control insect pests by eating them.

The carrion beetles live inside and on dead animals. Some beetles spend their entire life in the water. Smaller beetles are often found on plants and flowers.

**Right:
The colorful ladybird
(ladybug) beetle lives
on flowers and
plants.**

SENSES

Beetles have the same five senses as humans. Their eyesight is good. Many beetles rely on their eyesight to find food and mates. Fireflies use their lights to find their mates. Other beetles use sound to attract their mates.

Most of a beetle's sense organs are located on the head. But it also has hairs on the thorax, abdomen, and legs that are sensitive to vibrations. The antennae contain sense organs that are sensitive to vibrations and airborne smells.

**Right:
Notice this
longhorned beetle's
large black eyes and
long antennae.**

DEFENSE

Most beetles use camouflage to defend themselves. If they look like their surroundings, an enemy can't see them. Other beetles will bite an enemy.

Some beetles, like the ladybird beetles, have a hard set of wing covers that are too slippery for a predator to grab onto. Some ground beetles squirt a stream of burning acid onto an enemy. Other species squeak loudly and startle their enemy. Bright colors can be a defense as well. Brightly colored beetles usually taste bad.

**Right:
A ladybird beetle
is hard for a
predator to grab.**

**Left:
A stag beetle can
bite hard.**

FOOD

Beetles eat just about everything. Many are predators, and eat other insects. Ladybird beetles eat aphids, and are often used to control the pests. They can eliminate the need for insecticides.

Other species eat wood, and can damage buildings. Dutch elm disease is caused by bark beetles whose larvae tunnel under the bark and destroy elm trees.

Beetles also eat crops. The boll weevil can destroy a cotton field. The larvae cause the most problems. This is why farmers use insecticides.

**Right:
A May beetle
eating a plant.**

GLOSSARY

Abdomen (AB-do-men) - The rear body part of an arthropod.

Algae (AL-gee) - A plant without a stem that lives in the water.

Antennae (an-TEN-eye) - A pair of sense organs found on the head of an insect.

Arthropod (AR-throw-pod) - An animal with its skeleton on the outside of its body.

Camouflage (CAM-a-flaj) - The ability to blend in with the surroundings.

Ectothermic (ek-toe-THERM-ik) - Regulating body temperature from an outside source.

Environment (en-VI-ron-ment) - Surroundings in which an animal lives.

Fungi (FUN-guy) - Simple plants.

Habitat (HAB-uh-tat) - An area in which an animal lives.

Insect (IN-sekt) - An arthropod with three body parts and six legs.

Insecticide (in-SECK-tih-side) - A substance for killing insects.

Larva (LAR-vuh) - The second stage of an insect that goes through a complete metamorphosis.

Metamorphosis (met-uh-MORE-fuh-sis) - The change from an egg to an adult.

Order (OAR-der) - A grouping of animals.

Predator (PREAD-a-tore) - An animal that eats other animals.

Pupa (PEW-puh) - The third stage of an insect that goes through a complete metamorphosis.

Species (SPEE-seas) - A kind or type.

Thorax (THORE-axe) - The middle body part of an arthropod.

INDEX

About the Author

Jim Gerholdt has been studying reptiles and amphibians for more than 40 years. He has presented lectures and displays throughout the state of Minnesota for nine years. He is a founding member of the Minnesota Herpetological Society and is active in conservation issues involving reptiles and amphibians in India, Aruba, and Minnesota.

Photo by Tim Judy